# Spiritually Seeing

Photography by Constance Melahoures
Words by Judith Campbell

Riverhaven Books

*Spiritually Seeing* is a work of collaboration between the photographer and poet.

Published in the United States by Riverhaven Books, www.RiverhavenBooks.com

ISBN : 978-1-951854-03-4

Printed in the United States of America

Edited and designed by
Stephanie Lynn Blackman
Whitman, MA

Dedicated to those who see the beauty

# What Does it Mean to Spiritually See?

More and more often I hear people say, "I'm not very religious, but I'm very spiritual." When, as an ordained minister, I ask these same people what that means to them, they are often at a loss for words and turn to back to me for an answer.

N.B. There is no short answer for this question,
but what follows is a brief summation of how I respond.

\*\*\*

The spiritual life, for many, is not necessarily found in religious practice, or in a formal church setting. How we humans see, speak, listen, and elect to use our time to experience the world around us, our immediate, mundane, ordinary, dishwashing, walk the dog, clean up after the party world, can be a spiritual experience…if we want it to be. We can choose to open ourselves to the probability of being stopped in our tracks, and even called to action by an image, a thought, a word, a deed, or the kindness of a stranger. How we respond to these moments of insight is up to us. We can stop, look, listen, and be grateful and thoughtful, or we can blink and hurry on past to the next item to be ticked off the to-do list. Too often we allow ourselves to become human DOINGS, rather than human BEINGS.

\*\*\*

Connie Melahoures and I have several points of intersection in our daily lives in and around Plymouth, Massachusetts. We sing next to each other in a local chorus. We both love animals. We are active in our respective churches and work side by side in our local interfaith clergy alliance.

As you look at this book – it is a 'looking at' book – let yourself fall into the alternating rhythms of the words and the images, and then move into the harmony that comes from the two together. You might even come up with some words of your own…feel free to add them…there's loads of room for you, the reader, in these pages.

What we hope for you, in reading this book, is that you will begin to see your own ordinary and everyday world in a new way. That the beauty and harmony in the ordinary and the mundane will reveal itself to you….and when it does, you will stop and look and listen.

We wish you hours and days, and sometimes only fleeting moments, of spiritually seeing for yourself.

Connie Melahoures
(Rev.) Judy Campbell

Living the prayer, walking the prayer,
Breathing in and out –
All is the prayer

Run into the storm
Or away –
Your choice
But for now, let's just walk in the rain.

Sleep 'neath my wing, little one
Safe from the foxes and turtles
and man

Come be with me
While there's still time
Before I am only a memory

Be quiet, noisy, foolish, well-meaning poet.
You don't need words
This time.

River of gold
To a sea untold
My dreams on hold
Break free
And fly

If I painted this
Would you believe it?
Cranberries in October

Mating is…
Ungraceful
Messy
Sticky
And ordained by God…

All mouth baby bird
Soon, she'll feed her own younglings
If she lives that long

I gave you today
I cannot promise tomorrow
I'm only your mom

Hey, bird… you dropped this.
You don't want it?
Do you really think I can fly?

Fragile scarlet poppies grow
Wild, on Flanders Field
…and in my garden

We are called to this
To be present to the mystery
And to protect it.

Monarch of the garden
Your colors eternal
Your reign far too short

Be open to the sun, the rain, the dew
Bloom now
One day we will fade

Death and new life
The Yin and Yang of all existence
Side by side

Sea…stones…sand
Ever shifting over time
Thee, they, me, thou
We all move with the tide

Running water will shape a rock
Carve a valley
Nourish the trees
…and kill

Mayflowers
They named a big brave ship after you
…Who knew you were so small?

No one knew I was there,
Speaking, knowing, breathing
and being…the prayer

Listen to me, dammit!
Listen to me, please!
…How else will I know I exist?

Look up…look down…
One way is clear, one is not…
We live somewhere between the two

I see the moon,
The moon sees me.
Is this how
It's supposed to be?

Rock, sea, you, me.
Once was
Is now
And may yet be
Speak, while there's still time

(I ask...)
"What immortal, *hand or eye*
Could frame *thy fearful symmetry*."
(Wm Blake)

Fish hawk –
Fierce and faithful partner,
Tireless daddy osprey,
Death on wings

Sound and fury
Wings outspread
Hoarse, hissed warning me
…Don't mess with a swan.

One for sorrow,
Two for joy,
Three for a girl, and four for a boy,
But now I have to ask you this…
Whatever happens with five and six?

Outside dining
On the spot –
She loves me true
…or loves me not

Tired and hungry from tending the queen
The workers can feast
At last

Standing back to the wind
Ruffles all feathers
Turn and lean into it

"Since singing is so good a thing,
I wish all men would learn to sing."
(William Byrd, English Composer)

"Now the day is over,
  Night is drawing nigh;
  Shadows of the evening
  Steal across the sky."
                (Sabine Baring-Gould, 1834-1924,
                              Composer)